OFF
GUARD

First published 2003 by
Bradshaw Books, Cork, Ireland
This edition published 2024 by
Wordsonthestreet
Six San Antonio Park, Salthill, Galway, Ireland
web: www.wordsonthestreet.com
email: publisher@wordsonthestreet.com

The moral right of the author has been asserted.
A catalogue record for this book is available from the British Library.

ISBN 978-1-907017-68-1

Cover design, layout and typesetting: Wordsonthestreet

OFF
GUARD

TONY O'DWYER

WORDSONTHESTREET

Tony O'Dwyer grew up in Ennistymon, Co Clare and now lives in Galway. His poetry has been published in a wide variety of journals.

He has won a number of poetry competitions and was runner-up in the Patrick Kavanagh Award.

He is co-editor and publisher of *Crannóg* magazine.

His first collection was published by Bradshaw Books, Cork in 2003.

His next collection is due from Salmon Poetry in 2025.

Acknowledgements

Thanks to members of Galway Writers' Workshop, past and present, for their constructive criticism, advice and support.

Thanks to members of The Peer Group for their input, and for their inspiration and encouragement to publish this second edition of *Off Guard*.

Some of the poems in this collection have appeared in the following publications: *Podium I* and *II*, *Asylum*, *Books Ireland*, *Cúirt Journal*, *Poetry Ireland Review*, *Writing in the West*, *Crannóg*.

'And catch the heart off guard and blow it open.'
Seamus Heaney, *Postscript*

To my siblings
Pat and Mena

PREFACE

The first edition of *Off Guard* was published in November 2003 by Bradshaw Books of Cork.

A selection of the manuscript had won a place in the Patrick Kavanagh Award a short time previously and I entered much the same manuscript of twenty-five poems for the Bradshaw Books competition, and it won. That was twenty-one years ago.

The book became out of print and so having been a publisher now for most of those twenty-one years, and spent time publishing and promoting the work of others, I decided to give *Off Guard* a new lease of life.

In revising the text of *Off Guard* I made some minor edits to some of the poems. Sometimes this involved altering a word here and there, omitting a word, or simply making minor changes to punctuation. I excluded six poems. These were poems that I considered in hindsight to be below par and not salvageable by even major edits. This second edition now has forty-five poems instead of the original fifty-one.

The order of the poems follows for the most part a chronological path. The book opens with poems based on childhood experiences. It goes on to deal with teenage years, relationships and family, the passing of parents and what might be called the general concerns of approaching middle-age.

The poems were written over a period of about five years. Some came to me almost fully formed while others took longer. For example the poem about my sister *A House of Make Believe* took practically all of those five years, going through several iterations before I finally settled on the villanelle form. It had started out as an overly emotional poem so I think placing it within the confines of form helped to control that.

There are many other deeply personal poems in the book; poems of bereavement and of other losses and longings, and some of joy as well. There is *Stella Maris* a poem about my father's final days in the eponymous nursing home. There is *Roots*, about planting a tree with my young son. However I'm a believer in *la mort de l'auteur*, the poet's life is irrelevant to the meaning of the work. I believe poems are foremost constructs of the imagination and thus are fictions no matter how rooted in reality they may be.

Furthermore I'm a stylist. In any writing, whether poetry or fiction or memoir, my main preoccupation and focus is on language. Thus in poetry I strive to pay attention to imagery, sound, and form. So whether in my own poetry or in another's I'm less concerned about what the poem is 'about' than how it is presented linguistically.

The connection with music is strong. A piece of music is pure sound, the meaning is less in the musical piece and more invoked within the listener. In a poem words become notes, phrases become chords, a section of a poem can become a riff of suggestion and emotion, stanzas are like movements, and the entire poem should have the arc of a tune and its lines, or bars, should rise and flow and fall with the same sense of satisfaction.

I hope I have achieved this in some way and that these poems give you that same sense of satisfaction.

Tony O'Dwyer January 2024

CONTENTS

Memory

In the dry dust beneath snow-berry bushes
Hens scratched and pecked,
Rhode Island Reds, White Wyandottes, Light Sussex.

They sometimes laid out, as if in spite.
The eggs, hidden for weeks, would be found putrid,
Insides gurgling, the rot loosened.

I shattered them against the garden wall,
The white and yellow slime tracing wanton
Shapes through the twist of stones.

Six years old, crouching among the bushes,
Between thumb and forefinger I squeezed
A snow-berry, watched the white dribble ooze

From the cracked skin,
And a memory born.

Skating

Each winter the rains drained from Black Mountain,
Moving in stealthy rivulets through brown heather,
Cover of fern fronds;
Searching grim days, desolate nights for sodden fields
Where land levels, then hollows,

Making a silver pond
That grabbed the bright daytime sky,
Crushed the heat from it,
Licked the reedy edges, the rough hoof-printed clay,
Soaking our toecaps through.

One year it froze to a green translucence;
We skated end to end over stilled burdock,
Trapped chickweed,
Till hard stars gathered
Sending us home tingling through a chalybeate night.

In two days there was a thaw:
From the fading edges to the centre
Enchantment crumbled.
Each year I longed for its return,
But though the cold rain settled, it never would
Mutate the green tinged silver to solid lanthanum.

Cascades

After winter rain
Brown water burst
From pools upstream.
Then the cascades wore
Torrential dress.

June's thirst forced apart
The broad slate's robes,
Exposing her belly to the sun,
Stretched out like the long summer day

We crossed the river floor
From bank to bank,
Our bared feet
Tracing the lines of her shale skin,
Reading, perhaps, the river's song-words.
Unconscious of the gathering swell upstream
Threatening to wipe us clean.

Ear to the Ground

The West Clare Railway line cut through our field
Parting it like enemies.
Railway gates made customs posts
Where adults crossed when scheduled.

But closer to earth, we used other divinations:
An ear placed solidly on the track
Was a herald for the drum of wheel-beats,
Vatic pulses of entrancement.

A row of pebbles lined up on the rail,
Gathered lumps of limestone, schist or shale,
Bits of our world to test the trespasser. We caged
Ourselves behind the gate, exulting in uncertainty.

Round the bend, far down the line, the faint snore
Of rhythms gathered. Fury rising, down Foran's Incline,
It snaked into sight. Then with a thunderous iron roar
The flanged wheels triturated stone.

We climbed the gate, considered the remains,
Watched the last wagon swing through other lands,
As the gritty dust in trickling grains
Crawled warm and exquisite from our hands.

Seven Figures

That summer's day, had to be a Sunday.
My father only used his Kodak Hawkeye
On bright Sundays; weekdays did not photograph.

In a shorn field of pale stubble my younger cousin
And I astride a hill of hay, winched and braced
On the hayfloat by her brother, skilled at just fourteen.

My sister, standing, dress caught in the breeze,
Arm raised, warding off the light;
Behind, a blanket of amnesiac sky.

Moll, forehead white-starred, between the shafts;
Sailor, paw forever poised, entering
The frame. All of us stilled in innocent sepia.

And my father, absent, but for his long shadow
Stretching across a golden childhood meadow.

Son

You were the first fresh page of a story,
Replete with texture and smell and mystery:
The feather-touch of your hair,
The purr of your sleeping,
And later, laughter squealing from your core,
Your shriek when your head
Disappeared in the dark of a sweater,
Delight when it emerged
Through a neck getting tighter by the week,
The riddle of your hand
Lost in the sleeve of a coat,
Your weight in my arms
Summing you up,
The ease with which I carried you ...

Roots

You carried home from school
A short stick of willow-wood
In your five-year-old fist.

We picked a corner of the garden
To ease the fleshy twig
Into the moist yielding clay.

All winter its thread-roots
Groped in the gelid blackness
Choosing its own anchor points,
Supports against the sway
Of its now broad muscular limbs.

Wings

You kick-slide your sausage bag towards the check-in desk,
Guitar held firmly by your side, its stickers fresh
 – *Ban the Bomb, Save the Weed,* or is it *Whale* –
Band-aids salving wounds not yet endured.
Your excitement is as tense as its strings
Poised to release its music.

Outside another plane takes off in anger or regret.
I ask you again to check your ticket, passport, cash.
We are left with no more words to name this passing.
Our silence is a rest between two notes.

Departure times flicker on screens,
The escalator lifts you to Gate 18;
I remain your key-note
Watching you rise through a crescendo of mist
Into the high pitch of blue air.

My Mother Prepares Strawberries

My mother, in her prime, prepares dessert,
Bent over a can of strawberries,
Sunlight in her hair.
The hooded blade hooks the flanged lip
And bites through metal
With a single incisor mark.
Forefinger and thumb wind the butterfly wings
And the ribbed wheel grips the can's edge.
Gradually the can revolves, gashing itself.

Beneath the opening wound the blood appears
Sweet and cool.
Then the soft swimming globules,
Visceral sacs of red ripe skin,
Bob in the blood for a moment
Then plunge to the waiting bowl,
There to fester,
While she grows old with other burdens.

Timepiece

Propped on his desk my father's fat watch
Mirrors him,
Graven-faced and silver-backed.
Its figures stern,
Like Roman soldiers guarding the perimeter.
Solid-footed sentinels, spears erect, swords crossed,
Allegiant to the hour.

Each night he winds it slowly, careful not to over tighten.
And puts it by his bed.
Its ticking is his lullaby
Recounting days' narratives.
All night it keeps vigil, staring at his sleeping,
Breathing its seconds faithfully.

By day it measures his steps
Slowing to a shuffle.

Stella Maris

i.m. Willie O'Dwyer MPSI

In the foyer of the rest home,
Polished by the sisters,
A hands-clasped Virgin Mary greets the visitor:
Welcome to the world of the old;
Leave your rules at the door
With the hats and umbrellas.

Down the hall the urine-laden
Atmosphere makes the head giddy.
The dayroom is a sea of dark lolling.

You are dozing after dinner.
Beads of it string to your front.
At my touch you raise demented eyes
That a few months before
Deciphered a doctor's scrawl and made a cure
For someone else's sickness.

While I wait you recite the old mantras
And we each die a little.
When I leave, you're staring at the floor,
As if your star had fallen there.

Paddy

i.m. Paddy O'Dwyer

Your boot scrunch on the path those winter nights
Was a snapped twig in a dark wood.
The clap of the knocker, raised and lowered once,
Your name scratched across the page of the evening.

Winter danced on your overcoat in the glow of the kitchen,
Making a night-sky of stars.
When you shook it off, they died one by one,
Houselights dimming before the curtain parts.

Then you become a conjuror, drawing tales,
Like chains of motley handkerchiefs,
From pockets fashioned out of fable,
Or making music from any common thing.

After you died I shook the dust of dreams
From the threads of your overcoat, searched in pockets,
Bottomless as despair, for any fabulous thing
To tell me the magic had not fled in the dark of its old cloth.

A House of Make Believe

i.m. Mena O'Dwyer

A house of make-believe can hold no dread.
A tracery of stones made simple squares.
But doors were closing down inside your head.

Beneath the summer sycamores you played
With your doll, in velvet, lace and flaxen hair.
A house of make-believe can hold no dread.

You wore a poppet bracelet which you said
I pulled apart, then mended, for a dare.
But doors were closing down inside your head.

I broke the doll to find out how it cried.
It was a simple act; I didn't care.
A house of make-believe can hold no dread.

Years on I sat beside your hospice bed,
Heard your breath become a thinly whispered prayer.
But doors were closing down inside your head.

When the prayer became your final breath
I was wishing it could take you back to where
A house of make-believe can hold no dread,
But doors were closing down inside your head.

The Ghost Moths

Now, even after all are gone who'd ever
Called them souls in hell and pitied them,
The ghost moths hover at the glass,
Their ball-point eyes menacing the light
As if it, and not they, would be consumed.
Driven by the darkness from the moonless
Trees, they come in the heat of June nights.

Behind them in the garden the single hawthorn
My father shaped with secateurs opens
Its silent blossoms. Yellow eyes on stalks
Sweeten the blackness that creeps along the lawn,
Climbs the sleeping stone wall of the shed,
And, drifting further back, soaks the wild fields,
Dissolving them to inky nothingness.

Somewhere the new moon hides, waiting its chance
To fix me on its slow journey across
This tattered piece of brightening earth, until
Moon, moth and blossom scent are all that's left
Before the fetid blackness closes in.

Vanishing Point

Waiting at Ennis railway station one hazy
Summer, time hovered above our youth;
Were we destined east to Limerick
Or west to Galway and its grey city?
The years have made all that irrelevant.
I remember an old man with a brown paper
Parcel shuffled to the platform seat, and sat,
As if forever.

You had chestnut hair, you were beautiful.
To impress, or shock, you I jumped onto the tracks
And put my ear to a rail: There's no train coming yet.
You screamed Be careful, but I paid no heed;
That forever afternoon as I looked along the rails
Somewhere up ahead they seemed to meet.

Our New House

Course after course the rough walls grew,
Cleft with staring holes for weather and crows
To haunt, making a ruin in reverse
Of it. A shadow of its own death.

Each day we stood within the rising walls,
Breathing the acrid cement dust and lime,
Consulting with the builder. Reckoning
Widths and distances, the heights of shelves;

Counting power-points; imagining the debris
Giving way to colour and texture and time's
Constant loom weaving our livery.
Two lovers dressed to kill, we would wear

This suit with style, accessorised with flair,
Yet seeing in its swaddling-clothes, its shroud.

Translated from the Fabulous

We built a house of stone,
With a stout door.
We locked our love in.
We huffed and puffed just to prove
Nothing could move it.

Then we dreamed. And in our dream
We built a house of wood,
Exactly where the old had stood.
We huffed and puffed just to prove
Passion's fire could not consume it.

When we awoke our house
Was a house of straw,
Fragile as filigree.
Now we are afraid to huff and puff;
Our lost love howls in the doorway.

Furniture City: Saturday Afternoon

We have reached the age of renovation
Now that our boys have grown and learned
To keep their feet off coffee tables.

We've been here before, a lifetime ago,
Made a nest from these sticks.
Learned the language: *dralon, duvet, veneer.*

Now I watch you lost among lanes
Of three-piece suites, avenues of beds.
This second furnishing is a graver task,

Without the hope of youth, excitement of a plan ...
By day's end we choose: a sturdy cabinet
That may outlast our love.

I tender my credit card and wonder if
Our heart's purse can hold the cost
Of furnishing an empty nest.

Plateau

Our backyard stares like an old man waiting for death,
Remembering its paddling-pools and sand-pits;
Once it was terrain for Highwaymen, Cowboys;
It was The Great Plains; it was The Rockies;
Its shrubberies were Sherwood,
And one year it hosted The World Cup.

The gap in our neighbour's hedge
Is veiled by a tangle of Escalonia,
Where once the currencies of childhood were exchanged.
And we have climbed great heights to reach this plateau
Over any edge of which
We may fall.

Losing

The art of losing isn't hard to master – Elizabeth Bishop

Last night November winds agonised the house,
Circling the howling walls,
In search, maybe, of love's calmness.

This morning I watch the last leaves
Cling tenuously and golden against the westerly gale,
Pulled taut on thin defiant twigs, stubborn, contumacious.

Pale undersides flickering like far off stars,
Their brown veins strain to grip the slender wood.
Stems twist until the sinews snap.

Released to the wind, they dance to the music
Of remembered blossom or blindly huddle
In a corner of some clustering field.

The bony branches shake in protest,
Bereft, tight-lipped with bitterness.

The barbed-wire fence, slack with years,
Leans on its aging posts.

Against a grey enamelled sky
Dark smudges of cloud heave eastwards.

I am left, watching paint peel from this canvas
And scatter like the crumbled gold of stardust
Into the black depths of space.

Naming Your Skin

Out in the garden I'm gathering up the Fuchsia cuttings,
Heaping them with the Eryngium and Hydrangea
Barrowing to the compost heap,
Or foostering with the loose bits of the lawnmower,
Coming to grips with the Briggs and Stratton,
Engrossed in all the hard-edged tasks of husbandry.

Behind the bathroom window you undress to bathe.
Through the beads of glass shadows of your skin
Loom and fade; your beauty broken
Like a jigsaw waiting to be made.

I hear the shower door shut, the grate and squeak
Of taps and the hissing stream pour over
You; cascading down your shoulders,
Your spine, your breast curve,
Spreading out from the Trapezius,
Over the Deltoids, racing across
The broad Latissimus Dorsus,
Filling the dimples of the Sacrum,
Surging round Gluteus Maximus,
Spouting down the Biceps Femoris,
Trickling round the Tibia and Fibula,
Finally reaching the tips of the Phalanges.

I watch the water singing from the outlet
Carrying its song-words underground.
I bend to place my fingers under it;
I cup my palm to drink,
The name of your skin dissolving on my tongue.

Mapping Your skin

We broke bread at the kitchen table,
Each slice a soft bloodless tissue, clear as unripened fruit.
In the garden the Chestnut's leaves were dying inwards from the
edge.
The sun, diluted by the earth's strife, shivered and hunched low.

We had come to the strangest place.
The knife-teeth sank again through the loaf's hump
Carving yet another land, white and unexplored,
Until our world was a cascade of slices on a plate.

Later, counting the brown island marks of your back
Where it narrows to the isthmus of your waist,
I dreamed the knife-tip piercing skin,
The blade drawn down, like my finger
Caressing the pebbles of your spine,
Pencilling a line of opening flesh
Drawing it back like a peeled orange.

I spread your skin on the brown formica
Like a Mercator Projection and read you all at once;
My hands chart rhumb lines; plan voyages;
Commit your contours to memory.

I am Vespucci gazing with awe on an old land,
Creating a cartography of flesh, of white coasts and central plains,
What is hidden by the night-time of the body,
Revealed on the blazing page of our passion.

Some Day I'll Write a Sonnet on Your Back

Some afternoon in some motel or inn
As we languish after love upon a bed,
The sheets a gathered toga at your waist,
I'll write a sonnet on your delicate skin
With magic marker, preferably red.
Carefully from your shoulder in no haste
I'll draw the chiselled point across the thin
Papyrus from your buttocks to your head.

Between your shoulder blades I'll squeeze an octet,
A sextet in the hollow of your spine.
I'll use an oil-based ink so we can save
Forever the memory of each line,
A permanent reminder that we have
Love deeper than this mere skin-deep design.

Shadows & Jazz

The sound of a clarinet can seduce
Even the most careless of hearts
As the short pumping kisses of breath,
The deft curving of fingers,
Transform to hot melting notes.

We danced, holding our hands low,
The music swaying on our bodies,
Twined in senseless rhythm.

Jazz is so sensuous, you whispered,
And it seemed the notes, still in their music sheets,
Floated across the room to caress my skin.

Going home, under the pale light of a lamp post,
You stopped to consider our shadows,
Lying like two secrets on the sleeping street.

I can't remember if there were stars or a moon.
Or if there was only a blackened sky
And our dark shapes turning their backs,
As if we were standing behind two envied lovers
Transformed by the music, the light, and
Their own single, uncomplicated love.

Gracetime

It is like the twilight or the space we'd travelled
Through between cities, neither here nor there.

Pillars, arms of stone, hold the world above us
And make a nether land of thaumaturgy,

While buds of cherry blossoms sit like raindrops
On suburban branches, and in the

National Gallery strangers drift past
The Impressionists: bustled ladies linking

Arms with sombre, bearded men; coloured
Dashes codify a face, a wave,

A lighthouse, splendid blooms. They touch with eyes
What Monet touched but fail to understand

How distance fashions meaning from his palette;
Like in our cave of wonder below stairs

Your fingers touch my lips and cling, as if
The space between us is too much to bear.

Words

We walked a field where hazels stood gaunt and spare,
Their muscles tense against the February light.
Catkins dangled like quotation marks
Waiting to enclose our words. In the distance
A chainsaw screamed out for the wood it cut
Then died in the throat of invisible songbirds.

We searched among the ancient lettering
Of clints and grykes in limestone rocks
For a seat, smooth as the pauses in our talk.
You were as spare as the hazel,
As bright as the February light.
Your lips stopped my words as softly as catkins.

The Colour of Consonants

This, it seems, is the year for buttercups
With skin like yellow lycra
Incandescent in June sun.

They sprout taller than the hot, dry grass
Making me think it needs cutting,
Though it struggles in stunted raggedness.

So I set the blades high and
Shred their heads to a golden wind;
Wide-eyed petals stretch to ripe platinum.

I think of you boarding a plane
At Fiumicino airport, leaving a land
Where vowel sounds rip through the air.

And of the way you imitate my
Way of saying 'I don't know',
Putting the emphasis on the 'T',

Tipping the consonant with your tongue,
My initial that I never seem to clip, or lose
Among the uncertain openness of vowels.

Dreaming of Killadoon

Before I realised you'd ever lead another life,
I dreamed I was turning south from Louisbourg
And driving the endless road that skirts Mwealrea
To meet you on an afternoon in spring,
The sea on my right straining to kiss the shore,
The air heavy with half-promise.

By early twilight we had walked the beach,
Our footprints meandering among rocks.
The sea hissed at our falsehood
As we talked the moon into its prime
And met the dawn together,
A golden edge to a looming hill.
It was a clear dawn,
As if it were not the end of anything.

Cold Country

I imagine you going home from university
Through the vaporous cold,
The clatter of the tram emptying the streets for evening;
You sit grim against the grey Zurich damp.

Or rehearsing an end of term play
Among the ropes and climbing frames of a gymnasium,
The maple floor lined and arced for basketball,
White and blue tape lifts at points, is scuffed.

Outside, the neighbouring business district chews
On the buttered bread of the city.
Trams screech earnestly for attention.
Muffled pedestrians, hard-faced against the iron cold,

Are drawn towards some bleak point.
Soon, you, too, may travel home through tattered streets.

A Farmer's Journal

i.m. Peter Coyne, Roscam

All weathers have cut a harsh landscape
In the stone of his face,
Traversing his Atlantic-lashed farm,
Between field and barn at the world's edge.
Flocking, fencing, filling gaps in the hedge,

Winter catches him,
Shoulders canvas-bagged against the rain.
Gaunt hawthorns, fine-line drawn against a heartless sky,
Chronicle his burden
In nature's rough calligraphy.

Spring puts a spurt in his step, with calves, new growth,
Plough and harrow.
A dropped lamb in the crook of his arm,
Bottle-fed by the back door,
His shepherding's eternal.

Summer dresses him in sweat and a straw hat.
Meadows become his parchments.
Swathes falling to the fluency of his scythe,
Draw headlines for autumn's chaff
To follow through to the year's conclusion.

Galway Bay

On the horizon
The slow threat of rain.

A darkening on the water
Throws up excited gulls
Giving voice to a grey wave.

The bay is rolled in woollen folds,
Loosely wound
With strings of pewter.

I am touched by a chill that stirs memory:

Giant cliffs, ankle deep in a blistered sea;
Dense swirls of wind-raked Cord-grass;
The sharpness of salt on the breeze.

Now, through the mist,
Glimpses of infinite light.

Girl With Violin by the Eglinton Canal

The water, driven by weeks of rain,
Is giving a grand performance
In high misty octaves.
Overhead the sun has polished the sky;
Light slips onto the canal;

A young woman is playing a violin.
Music like the scent of apples
Sweetens the lock's fall.
Each note a petal floating,
Creamy edges, roseate centres.

The afternoon spins on the tension of a string.
The air crystallises to refulgent sound.
The water applauds, flinging kisses
Like blossoms
Into the steel yellow day.

Tourists

In the hotels tourists are busy at breakfast.
Eating new breads as if sampling a native custom.
Or an unfamiliar language being slowly learned.
Soon they will enter a new city
And see, like innocents, houses, offices, corner shops.
Hear the odd wheezings of buses filled with
People as strange as a new invention,
Travelling to unimaginable places.

The city is like a map torn at the edges.
Streets trail off into possibilities.
They step over the cracked lines
From fold to fold, where words peel away,
And there is a kind of darkness, a loss.

They drift into the market place,
Eyes like ancient currencies
Proffered and withdrawn from stall to stall,
Acquiring the mantle of the travelled
Become their own souvenirs,
Minds broadened, world narrowed.

Suburb

Residential road, autumn afternoon. Crisp.
A woman waits at a bus-stop,
Tweed skirted and gloved. Leaves at her feet.

Behind her, mellow sycamores
Squint in the pale October light,
Their arms strong enough
To hold a grand-child's swing.

Everything waits here in the afternoon.
Waits and dreams.
But the heart pumps:
Its life-blood a gust of breeze; a swirl of leaves;
The flux and fade of a passing car;
The clack-clack of a jackdaw; silence;
The trees' whispering; echoes;
A maid's polishing in a distant drawing-room;
A hush of memory; the creak of time passing;
The woman waiting.

The moment is middle-aged,
Poised between time and timelessness,
Toppling forward always, even in its stillness.

The gloved hand is raised.
The trees stretch their arms to the strengthening wind,
Lamenting their rootedness,
And offer their fruit in return
For the comfort of a child's play.

But the leaves dare not listen to the trees' sigh
As they skip contentedly towards winter,
Lest they learn that the truth lies
Not in the leaves nor in the branches,
But in the space between,
In the wrenching of the leaves by the passing breeze.

Painting a Room

The three-piece suite sits self-consciously
In the centre of the room,
Embarrased to reveal
What it's been hiding behind its back.
I cover its shame in drop-cloths.

A brisk sweep clears
The conscience of the skirting:
Misshapen residues of spider webs.
I pocket the five-penny piece,
Save the soldier, the marble, the wheel
And the possibly useful plastic pieces.

The carpet stares at me in terror,
Trapped in its snug fit.
I soothe it with newspapers;
Yesterday's, last week's and some from April.

The sheets shoulder each other. Still keen.
Headlines, used to prominence,
Gasp dying news:
Rumours of war; celebrities in town; political stances;
Old heroes pose and wave on the floor,
Oblivious to the daubs and smears, until,
By tea-time, they're bundled in a black body-bag,
And crumpled to undignified history.

Meanwhile the walls shine.
Their time has come.

Florists: February Fourteenth

Men,
having knocked off from the building sites
And assembly plants, parked the forklift,
Bundled up the tools, flock to the flowershop
To buy the obligatory bouquet. Shotgun petals.

Beer-swollen bodies bursting through acrylic,
Arms folding nervously, unfolding,
Feet tapping, teeth sucking,
Doing the annual florist's floor shuffle,
Queue, sheepishly, to stem-snipping counter girls
(The only girls who'll give flowers today)
Creating sprays, displays, bouquets,
Bunches of promise blossom, freesia drips,
Scissors-happy assistants
Stifling the sap from the bloom
Performing botanic vasectomies,
Ensuring endless, fruitless, floral sex.

Finally, men
emerging, bouquet held downwards
Like an implement, limply, but sheathed, prepared,
Duck to waiting cars and home;
Women win garlands,
Laurels to linger another year on.

But the message inside the flowers is blank.
Love is snipped in the bud!

The Clean Hero

The first time I saw Swarfega
Was on a summer job in a Midland town,
The Stratford Plant & Tool,
A greasy joint.
I was twenty-one years old and had read the works of Shakespeare.
In the toilet of the Stratford Plant & Tool
I tried it out,
This green jelly with the strange name.
It dissolved the day's accumulation,
Miraculously.
Small wonder it merited that medal for quality.

On the way home to the digs I was accosted by Boot-Boys,
Who didn't give a shit about the works of Shakespeare,
Or the cleansing properties of Swarfega.
My stomach churned, my legs jellied, my face greened
As they circled menacingly.
My cleansed fists held out no hope of defence.
But miraculously they left me intact,
Confused in my cowardice.
Medals are not easily merited.

Checkout

I don't know how long you've waited at this pier
For me to dock my netted catch of groceries;
How many Branflake boxes bleeped past you
Until your eyes glazed over like two frozen peas
And your left arm ached
From swinging over the same old record?

I only know that, when my Next Customer bar
Slid to a halt at your poised and painted fingertips
And you checked out all my twenty-six items
Without once raising your long and lovely lashes,

(Until, that is, you handed me my till receipt
Which told me you were operator twenty-four
And thanked me for shopping in the store
And asked me to please call again)

You could have played Lana Turner
To my William Wilkerson!

Recreation Excerpt

. . . For days our alma mater loomed
Like the start of any term. Beginning
In the pit of the stomach, ending in
High vaulted hallways, whose echoes whispered
Once again like hushed admonishments.
Fat and grey, (like Hall and Knight!),
We had returned, maybe been recaptured,
Like after any other term's escape;
Brought back to memorise forgotten lines
Translated by a vague remembered grammar.

We searched each other for identities
As if for bodies buried under debris
Of toppled towers, robbed from us in too
Many recreations, knowing that
Life's as much a quest for what's been lost
As of the turning of the bow towards Ithaca
Where fumbling with the sails of destiny
We recreate our own forgetfulness . . .

Breaking Fast

Eight a.m. and the radio's concerns,
Hatred, envy, deceit, a little joy,
Break through the vague fissures of dawn
To mingle with the disarray of breakfast things:

Toast crusts lying in their own flaked skin;
Marmalade shreds curling like rotted entrails;
Tea stains, contagious blotches; a splintered eggshell
Holding on to some old memory.

There is a finality in our first acts
Until we leave behind these shards
To crawl through the incisions
Snakelike into the sun,

While the radio continues to repeat
Whatever it had said.

On Reading Buck Mountain Poems

i.m. Anne Kennedy

When I read of the San Juan Islands
Folded into Juan de Fuca Strait
And Orcas shaped like the whale
Where your sunswept farm edged the Pacific,

I thought of how you lie on a hill in Rahoon
Under a right Galway drizzle,
And how raindrops dance through the air,
Swirling and spiralling, until they land
On any one of a million melting places;

Or, is it that the space through which they fall
Is so precisely measured that they each find,
After all, their one true spot on which to rest?

Sunday in Coole

While Sunday walkers were at their work-a week
Someone civilised the grassy verge;
Amputated limbs to better shape a tree;
Planned new paths through Coill na Chnó;
Left the logs all neatly stacked and then
Placed arrowed signs to point our steps away
From where they watch and wait:
Shy Dryads at rest among the leaves.

Night Watching

The Dublin train rattles into the night,
A night-bird screech splitting the night air.
The landscape is moon washed,

Time passes, bearing hour to hour.
Clock-face teases wakefulness.
Suddenly world turns,
Moon drops.
Appallingly, familiar light
Gives a slow burgeoning tap on my window-blinds
And draws me towards day.

Testament

My presence disturbs the arid
Air, unused to human agitation.
Objects fear my unfamiliar steps
Trespassing their years of steadfastness.
Dust, long at peace, unsettles.

In the attic space I find the chest,
Its metal bands pocked with mottled rust,
And lower it gently through the narrow door.

Steadied on the floor I turn the worn
Key; it clicks, I raise the bowed lid and
Discover ragged pages, wrinkled folds
Of surviving skins, generations old,
Lying like their signatories in caskets.

I unfold the fragile bones, peel back the skin,
Delicately hold the shreds of membranes,
To reveal the coursing blood of past disquiets:

Frail voices speak of Mortgages and Deeds, Titles, Boundaries,
Appurtenances, unbending words,
Inscribed with ornate letters of the law, by clerks
Who chronicle the text and lend their signatures
As witnesses to the passing round, and on, of little plots.

Ancestral names flourish at the end
Affirming both assent and character.
My fingers trace the shapes of signatures
To add my testament to these frayed pages,
Their crumbled fragments swirling in the air.

Vertices

I

Late November at the fall of night,
The first stone chippings are scattered on the sky:
Charon, Vega, resilient Venus.

Around me the muscles of the earth tense,
Anticipating the night with its fierce potentiality for love.
Lips quiver, *Wish upon the Evening Star.*
Across the moor the land squelches and winks;
The mountain pines have caught a fat moon in their nets;
Somewhere a dog barks out a confession or a prayer.

On a pale hill a single gorse is twisted with loneliness,
Leader or outcast from the barely tolerable gathering at the
foothills.
Stringed fenceposts, sunken and out of tune
Bend towards some secret lodestone.
And look! Someone has paved the road ahead with ladles of
mercury.
Darkness pours out as if casting a death-mask.

Beyond the lip of glowering hills,
Where the light falls like a dish of Eastern fare,
You sit at an upstairs window.
Venus rolls her eye in your direction
Reminding you that love exists, sometimes momentarily,
Endures even, or is endured.

You look out on fields linked by gaps of tumbled walls,
Prints of tractor wheels, stitching moments.
Hooks and eyes keep us fastened up,
Steadfast, maybe, respectable, possibly;

II
A unicorn comes prancing on the lawn,
Out of the almond moonlight.
The text of night grows larger, clearer.
The pictures, on the other hand, blur,
Like shadowy woodcuts.
From half-glimpsed shrubberies comes lyre music

Such as Orpheus played for his Euridyce
And made the awestruck Hades give her back
To lose again for one impassioned glance.
Enchantment turns your flesh to water;
You are an ivory stream, with ruffling birds,
A bending unicorn, the eye of Venus, on you,

On me. The road is carved with lovers' names,
Long dead, weathered to vague lines,
A history threading through the earth's rough skin.
In the bogland lake pine trees are hung by the heels,
Where tonsured mountains bathe their ancient wounds,
Scabs of stone healed with lambent silver.

And what now of the wish and the quivering lips?
The sky is full, the air is clear.
We embrace a tortured miracle.